COLORADO

MICHAEL WELCH

THE HISTORY OF THE

ROCKIES

CREATIVE EDUCATION

Published by Creative Education
123 South Broad Street, Mankato, Minnesota 56001
Creative Education is an imprint of The Creative Company

Designed by Rita Marshall
Editorial assistance by John Nichols

Photos by: Allsport Photography, Corbis-Bettmann, Fotosport, SportsChrome.

Library of Congress Cataloging-in-Publication Data

Welch, Michael, 1963–
The History of the Colorado Rockies / by Michael Welch.
p. cm. — (Baseball)
Summary: A history of the team that brought major league baseball to the
Rocky Mountain region of America.
ISBN: 0-88682-907-0

1. Colorado Rockies (Baseball team)—History—Juvenile literature.
[1. Colorado Rockies (Baseball team)—History. 2. Baseball—History.]
I. Title. II. Series: Baseball (Mankato, Minn.)

GV875.C78W45   1999
796.357'64'0978883—dc21   97-46395

First edition

9 8 7 6 5 4 3 2 1

Denver, Colorado, is a bustling metropolis of 500,000 people nestled at the foot of the scenic Rocky Mountains. Because of the extreme altitude of its location, Denver has long been known as the "Mile High City," and its history goes back to the early days of the American West.

Many of Denver's citizens are people originally from other parts of the country who have come to Colorado's capitol city to reap the rewards of the area's strong economy and beautiful scenery. Denver is a city with many diversions. Its mild climate features warm, pleasant summers followed by snowy yet temperate winters. Skiing, hiking, and outdoor

Third baseman Charlie Hayes.

The Colorado front office unveiled the team logo and announced the franchise's name, the "Rockies."

activities of all kinds are very popular among the city's residents, but Denver's biggest source of entertainment may come from its professional sports teams. The Mile High City is home to football's Denver Broncos, basketball's Denver Nuggets, hockey's Colorado Avalanche, and, since 1993, the Colorado Rockies.

In their short history, the Rockies have become one of professional sports' biggest success stories. Denver had long been a minor league baseball town—dating back to the turn of the century, when the city was home to the Denver Bears. The Bears competed in various minor leagues off-and-on until 1984, when the team was renamed the Zephyrs. Denver fans backed their minor-league teams vigorously, but all the while longed for a big-league team to call their own. As Denver's population exploded in the 1970s and '80s, the call for a major-league franchise grew louder and louder. Finally, in 1991, an ownership group led by trucking magnate Jerry McMorris put together an expansion package that was too attractive for major-league baseball to pass up. On July 5 of that year, the owners of the existing 26 big-league teams voted to award expansion franchises to Denver and South Florida. The Colorado Rockies and the Florida Marlins were born, marking the first expansion in the National League since the Montreal Expos and San Diego Padres joined in 1969.

LEADERSHIP COMES TOGETHER

The Rockies' front office had a lot of work to do between that proud moment in July 1991 and Opening Day 1993.

Rockies ace pitcher Pedro Astacio.

The Rockies nabbed Atlanta Braves pitcher David Nied with the first pick in the expansion draft, which was held November 17.

First and foremost, the team had to have a place to play. A site in Denver's lower downtown had been selected for the baseball-only stadium, but construction wouldn't be finished until 1995, and the Rockies and Marlins were supposed to begin play in 1993. The Colorado team arranged to play its first two seasons at the Broncos' home, Mile High Stadium, while the new facility, to be called Coors Field, was under construction.

Second, the Rockies needed personnel. Job one for general manager Bob Gebhard was to find someone to lead the team on the field. As a member of the Minnesota Twins' staff, Gebhard had helped assemble teams that won the World Series in 1987 and again in 1991. In 1987, a key trade had brought accomplished slugger Don Baylor to Minnesota from Boston. Baylor lent his cool confidence to the '87 Twins. When it came time to pick the Rockies' first manager, Gebhard recalled Baylor's leadership. Even though Baylor had not managed a professional team at any level, Gebhard asked the former American League Most Valuable Player to be the Rockies' on-field boss. Baylor accepted, becoming only the third black manager in the majors at the time.

"I didn't know if he could manage," Gebhard said. "He'd never managed a day in his life, but I thought if there ever was an opportunity for someone to step into a manager's role and learn, it would be with an expansion ballclub. So I took a chance on Don, and it certainly worked out."

One particular statistic from Baylor's 19-year career with Baltimore, Boston, Oakland, California, the New York Yankees, and Minnesota hints as to why Baylor has been successful as the Rockies' skipper. No major-leaguer in history has been hit by more pitches than he was during his playing career—Baylor took one for his team 267 times. The man is not intimidated by challenges.

A couple more stats from Baylor's playing career indicated things to come. He is one of only 10 players in history to rack up more than 250 home runs and 250 stolen bases in a career. With Baylor, the Rockies would be an offense-minded team.

The Rockies played their first home game in Mile High Stadium on April 9 to a record crowd.

GEARING UP FOR A MAJOR OFFENSE

Long before the Rockies began play, fans and sportscasters began talking about the effect of Denver's altitude on how far batted balls traveled and how little pitchers' breaking balls broke. The city is at the foot of the Rocky Mountains, a mile above sea level, so the air is thinner. Thrown or batted balls go about nine percent farther than they would in any other major-league city.

When Gebhard and his staff began putting the team together, they had to keep the thin-air phenomenon in mind. "We knew going into the expansion draft that Denver and its light air were certainly very conducive to hitters. So we knew we wanted to put together a powerful team as best we could under a limited budget," Gebhard says. The Rockies knew that with a team of hitters they could win some games in their first season and provide fans with exciting baseball.

On the other hand, building a pitching staff would be

The "Big Cat," Andres Galarraga.

Solid reliever Darren Holmes.

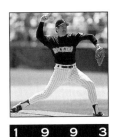

Bryn Smith claimed the first victory by a Rockies pitcher, 11–4 over Montreal on April 9.

extra tricky for the Rockies, because what makes Denver great for hitters makes it bad for breaking-ball pitchers. The thin air prevents the ball from moving as dramatically as it does at lower altitudes. Rockies management knew it would take a long time to develop a roster of hurlers whose stuff worked at high altitudes. "Pitching has always been a priority here, and it always will be," Gebhard said. "We have drafted a lot of pitchers and will continue to."

The expansion draft took place in November 1992. The Rockies and the Marlins took turns building their rosters by selecting players from other teams. The new teams couldn't just take anybody they wanted, though—the other major-league teams would make only a few players available for the draft, and they weren't about to give up their stars. Still, the Rockies managed to pick up several players who became cornerstones of the new team: infielders Eric Young from the Los Angeles Dodgers; Charlie Hayes from the New York Yankees; and Vinny Castilla from the Atlanta Braves' roster; veteran starter Kevin Ritz from the Detroit Tigers; catcher Joe Girardi from the Chicago Cubs; and pitchers with potential Steve Reed and Darren Holmes.

The Rockies also got key players for their debut team via other methods. The day before the expansion draft, they signed first baseman Andres Galarraga as a free agent. and traded for Dante Bichette, a journeyman whom Don Baylor had coached and liked when both men were with the Milwaukee Brewers. Baylor had worked with Galarraga in the past, too. When he was a coach for the St. Louis Cardinals, Baylor had helped a slumping Galarraga turn his career around. Baylor felt both Bichette and Galarraga had offensive potential that could explode into a lot of home runs in Denver's thin air.

First baseman Andres Galarraga became the Rockies' first-ever All-Star, going hitless in one at-bat during the game.

It didn't take long for the Rockies' hitting stars to shine in Colorado. The team finally played its first home game on April 9, 1993. Though the Rockies had lost their first two games on the road, their home debut was one for the record books. For starts, the biggest crowd to watch a baseball game—anywhere, ever—showed up. Mile High Stadium was packed with 80,227 fans eager to witness the first regular-season major-league baseball game to be played in the Mountain Time Zone. The attendance that day broke a

Speedy outfielder Alex Cole.

13

Reliever Steve Reed set the Rockies' record for appearances by a rookie with 64.

league record that had stood since 1958. People who had never seen a big-league game before came from as far away as Nebraska, Wyoming, and even Montana to see the Rockies battle the Montreal Expos.

Colorado did not disappoint those who made the trek for the team's home debut. In the Rockies' first home at-bat in history, second baseman Eric Young gave fans a taste of things to come when he homered off Montreal's Kent Bottenfield. The Rockies went on to win 11–4.

The first game's attendance didn't prove to be a fluke. Baseball fans kept on coming from near and far, helping the Rockies set an all-time season attendance record of 4,483,350.

Colorado's offensive assault didn't stop after the first night. The team piled up the runs at Mile High Stadium and compiled a 67–95 record for the season, setting a National League record for most wins by a first-year expansion team and giving the thin-air theorists plenty of fodder for their complaints about what Denver's altitude was going to do to the National League's record book.

Many people gave the thin air credit for Galarraga's improvement—he hit a league-leading .370 with 22 homers and 98 RBIs during his first year in Colorado. But Galarraga, who had been known as the "Big Cat" since his minor-league days because he is a large but nimble fielder, had started coming out of a hitting slump the year before he came to the Rockies. "Don [Baylor] helped me a lot with my mechanics in St. Louis," said Galarraga. "But most of all, he was a friend I could talk to. When he brought me here and told me I was his first baseman, I told myself I couldn't let him down."

Slick-fielding shortstop Walt Weiss.

Catcher Joe Girardi anchored the defense.

Bichette hit .310 with 21 homers and 89 RBIs in his first year in Colorado and hit the Rockies' first-ever home run—which came on the road at Shea Stadium in New York. Also stung by thin-air comments, Bichette credits his exceptional performances at the plate in the Rockies' first five seasons to the confidence Baylor has shown in him. "It doesn't matter if he's playing in Mile High, Coors Field, or the Grand Canyon, Dante's going to hit 'em out," the manager noted.

1 9 9 4

Bruce Ruffin got help from David Nied and Darren Holmes in recording the Rockies' first-ever shutout, blanking Philadelphia 5–0 April 14.

In its second season, the team was improving on most of its statistics—continuing to rack up impressive offensive numbers while cutting back on the number of runs they gave up—when the baseball strike cut short the 1994 season and forced cancellation of the World Series. Even with the shortened season, Galarraga and Bichette put up huge numbers: Bichette had a .304 average, 27 homers, and 95 RBIs, and Galarraga had a .319 average, 31 homers, and 85 RBIs.

While exciting to watch, the Rockies' offensive outburst did not translate into winning records in the team's first two seasons. Even though they outscored their opponents in both campaigns, the Rockies compiled a 120–159 record.

Things were different, though, when Colorado finally came home for good.

BLAKE STREET BOMBERS BRING WINNING HOME

The Rockies' huge attendance figures encouraged management to add 7,000 more seats to Coors Field before it opened. It also allowed the team to sign more free agents. By the time Coors Field was ready for action, the Rockies had added players who helped solidify Baylor's team. Steady

Outfielder Ellis Burks jolted many opposing pitchers (pages 18-19).

17

Pitcher Marvin Freeman led the Colorado club with 10 wins and an impressive 2.80 ERA.

defensive shortstop Walt Weiss and powerful outfielder Ellis Burks came over for the 1994 season (though Burks was injured for most of it), and Larry Walker signed with Colorado before the 1995 season.

Walker has made perhaps the biggest impact on the team. Since breaking in with the Expos in 1988, he has established himself as one of the best right fielders in the league. In his first year in Denver, he hit .306, belted 36 home runs, and knocked in 101 runs.

1995 also turned out to be a breakthrough season for third baseman Vinny Castilla. After never hitting more than nine home runs in any of his five previous professional seasons, Castilla belted 32 round-trippers with 90 RBIs and a .309 average in 1995. "Geez, what got into Vinny?" joked Baylor. "We always thought he could hit, but man, he's acting like Babe Ruth out there."

It was Bichette, though, who proved to be the hero as the Rockies broke in their beautiful new ballpark on April 26, 1995. The right-handed slugger launched a dramatic three-run homer to push Colorado past New York 11–9 in the 14th inning of the first game ever at Coors Field. It was the first of many crushing blows to be hit at Coors, and it ushered in the era of the "Blake Street Bombers"—big-league swingers Bichette, Galarraga, Burks, Castilla, and Walker. (The group takes its name from the ballpark's Denver street address.)

Bichette's performance in the Coors Field debut was just the beginning of an incredible season. He hit at a .340 clip and racked up a league-leading 128 RBIs and 40 home runs, coming in second in the voting for NL Most Valuable Player. More importantly, his run production helped the

Rockies to a 77–67 record, which earned them a wild-card spot in postseason play in only their third season.

ROCKIES CATCH POSTSEASON FEVER

Vinny Castilla had a breakthrough year, sprouting home run muscle (32) to join the "Blake Street Bombers."

In the playoffs, the Rockies faced the mighty NL East champion Atlanta Braves. In game one, before 50,040 frenzied Coors Field faithful, the Rockies held a 3–1 fifth-inning lead, only to see the Braves rally to win the contest 5–4. In game two, Colorado led 4–3 going into the top of the ninth before the Braves battered the Rockies' relievers for four runs and a 7–4 victory.

Down two games to none, most baseball experts thought the upstart Rockies would simply cave in and be swept in

Rockies starting pitcher Bill Swift.

Speedy infielder Eric Young.

three straight when the series moved to Atlanta, but the Rockies weren't done yet. Home runs by Eric Young and Vinny Castilla propelled Colorado to their first-ever postseason win, 7–5. The Rockies had struck a blow, but Atlanta came back the next night, eliminating the Rockies with a 10–4 victory. "It's been quite a run," said a smiling Don Baylor afterward. "Atlanta is the better club, but our guys really played hard. This experience is something we hope to build off of." Baylor was rewarded for his effort by being named the 1995 NL Manager of the Year.

With the Rockies' exciting run to the postseason fresh in their memories, Colorado fans held high hopes for the 1996 season. Unfortunately, fate dealt the team some cruel cards. A hustling Larry Walker crashed into a Coors Field fence while attempting to catch a long fly ball and was out of commission for much of the rest of the season. The Rockies' pitching staff, never a strong point, was wracked by injuries. Staff ace Bill Swift's shoulder problems continued from 1995, shelving the right-hander for all but 18.1 innings in 1996. Rockies' pitchers posted a 5.59 ERA—easily the worst mark in the league and also the worst ever by a Colorado staff.

The Blake Street Bombers, minus Walker, still packed plenty of punch, however. Galarraga led the league in homers and RBIs with 47 and 150. Burks hit .344 with 40 homers, 128 RBIs, and 32 stolen bases. Bichette hit .313 with 31 homers and 141 RBIs, and Castilla belted 40 homers, hit .304, and drove in 113 runs.

The awesome production by the Bombers left baseball historians scrambling to find a foursome of hitters who had ever done so well. Only the Steve Garvey-led 1977 Dodgers

1 9 9 5

Outfielder Dante Bichette socked homers in five consecutive games from August 1–5 to set a club record.

could boast four hitters with 30 or more home runs, and only the Hank Aaron-led 1973 Atlanta Braves can list three hitters with 40 or more. "Their numbers are just staggering," said Atlanta Braves manager Bobby Cox. "God help us if they ever get any pitching."

Never did the Rockies display their brutish offense and lack of pitching more vividly than during a late June series when they hosted the Los Angeles Dodgers. The Rockies won three of the four games, but the offensive explosion was astonishing. Colorado outscored the Californians by a total of 52–33, while combined, the two teams hit 25 home runs. They hit 10 in one of the wildest series finales in history, which lasted more than four hours even though it didn't go into extra innings. Colorado's Eric Young stole six

1 9 9 5

Starting pitcher Bill Swift led a struggling pitching staff by winning a club-record seven consecutive games.

Valuable starter Kevin Ritz.

bases in the game, and the Rockies won 16–15 by scoring two runs in the bottom of the ninth inning. In its 1996 wrap-up, *Sports Illustrated* magazine called this contest the "signature game" of the year in baseball.

Pitcher Armando Reynoso picked off eight base runners in the season to set a Rockies record.

WALKER SOCKS 'EM A MILE HIGH

After the offensive frenzy of 1996, Denver-area fans were hoping the Rockies could trade in some of their glossy offensive statistics for more team victories. "The only people who care about your individual stats are your agent and your mother," quipped Baylor. "This is America, and winning is all that counts."

The Rockies' powerful offense was strengthened even further with the return of a healthy Larry Walker. "It hurt to not be able to help the team as much as I would have liked last year," noted the star outfielder, who still hit 18 homers with 58 RBIs in only 83 games in 1996. "I'm really excited about getting back out there full time."

Walker must have been excited, because his performance in 1997 was simply one of the finest ever put together by any major-leaguer. The Canadian-born slugger flirted with hitting .400 for more than half the season before throttling back to end up at .366. He also pounded 49 homers, drove in 130 runs, stole 33 bases, scored 143 runs, and banged out 208 hits. "What he's doing is incredible," said San Francisco Giants All-Star outfielder Barry Bonds. "People will have to wait a few years and then look back on this to appreciate what he's done." Not surprisingly, Walker ran away with the 1997 National League MVP award.

1997 NL MVP Larry Walker (pages 26-27).

Fleet-footed second baseman Eric Young stole 53 bases to set a Rockies record.

The rest of the Blake Street Bombers also added to the fireworks with Galarraga blasting 41 homers and driving in a league-leading 140 RBIs and Castilla belting 40 round-trippers with 113 RBIs. Burks pounded 32 homers with 82 RBIs, and Bichette chipped in 26 circuit-shots and 118 RBIs. "We were all just trying to keep up with Larry," laughed Bichette. "We didn't want him to embarrass us."

Walker's spectacular season helped steer the Rockies back on a winning path, as the team stayed in the playoff hunt until the 158th game of the season. Colorado's 83–79 record marked the second winning season in the team's five-year history. "It's a positive step for us, sure," said steady reliever Steve Reed. "But we still have the same old problems. We have to pitch better." The team took a step in the right direction by acquiring hard-throwing right-hander Pedro Astacio in a midseason trade with the Los Angeles Dodgers. With Bill Swift still not completely back from his injury problems, Astacio gave Colorado a top starter to count on. Also, the team received solid performances from starter Roger Bailey and relievers Mike DeJean and Reed. Even with the improvement, Colorado pitchers still posted the league's worst ERA at 5.25. "The ballpark has something to do with it," noted Baylor. "But we still have to upgrade our pitching in order to see real success."

ROCKIES PLAN POSTSEASON BREAKTHROUGH

In the franchise's early years, the Rockies had to import players to compete in the National League, but now the team's farm system is starting to produce. Top prospect first

"Blake Street Bomber" Vinny Castilla.

Rising star, shortstop Neifi Perez.

Rocky Mountain slugger Dante Bichette.

1 9 9 8

After Jerry Dipoto's team-leading 16 saves the previous year, fans were anticipating another season of exciting play.

baseman Todd Helton has shown such great promise in the minors that the Rockies chose not to re-sign Andres Galarraga after the 1997 season. "Andres is 36 years old, and Todd is 24," explained Baylor. "Todd has a great future ahead of him. We'll miss Andres, but we have to think ahead." Also in the Rockies' future is young shortstop Neifi Perez, who hit .291 in 83 games with the big club in '97. Perez will team with free-agent acquisition second baseman Mike Lansing to form a solid double play combination for years to come.

On the pitching front, the Rockies scored a major victory by obtaining free agent hurler Darryl Kile from the Houston Astros. The right-handed Kile had a brilliant 1997 campaign in Houston, going 19–7 with a 2.57 ERA and 205 strikeouts. "With Darryl [Kile] and Pedro [Astacio], we think we now have as good a one-two pitching combination as anybody in baseball," said general manager Bob Gebhard. "If the young guys like [Roger] Bailey and [John] Thomson can come around, we'll be right there."

With the pitching corps upgraded and some new talent injected into the offense, Rockies fans will be cheering for a team with a bright future. At last, baseball's most potent hitting machine may finally be linked with a pitching staff talented enough to carry the Rockies deep into the postseason. "I don't make predictions," said Baylor, "but this is a pretty good ballclub."

For the faithful Colorado fans, the dream of a Rockies' championship may not be too far from reality. With the Blake Street Bombers, anything is possible, including a Mile High World Series.